BURDENS OF A DREAM

BURDENS OF A DREAM

33 Actionable Nuggets of Wisdom for the Creative Entrepreneur

Craig M. Chavis Jr.

AUTHOR ACADEMY elite

Printed in the United States of America.

Published by Author Academy Elite

P.O. Box 43

Powell, OH 43065

www.authoracademyelite.com

Library of Congress Control Number: 2019918566

ISBN: 978-1-64746-021-1 (Paperback)

ISBN: 978-1-64746-022-8 (Hardback)

ISBN: 978-1-64746-023-5 (eBook)

Available in paperback, hardback, e-book, and audiobook.

Creative Direction and Book Design by Craig M. Chavis Jr.

Cover Design by Jon McGregor and Debbie O'Byrne

www.burdensofadream.com

Dedication

This book is dedicated to all those who'll dare to answer their calling to abandon the status quo, follow the road not taken, and discover the person they're truly meant to become.

Table of Contents

Acknowledgments

One ironic thing about life is that no matter how hard you try, you can never run away from yourself. For years, I struggled with my past and continually questioned why things happened the way they did. I figured writing a book would remedy this process, yet, there were days when I wanted to forget everything, ignore my thoughts, and leave this project in the dust.

Thankfully, I had an excellent support system, and without the following individuals, it would have been impossible to bring this book into fruition:

Mom, Dad, and Celeste – I am truly blessed to call you family, and without you three, I would not be where I am today. Thanks for the guidance, unconditional love, and all the support.

John and Debbie – you two are fantastic visual artists. It was a pleasure working with you and thanks for brilliantly illustrating my vision on the book covers.

Mr. Mills and Dr. Miller – thanks for all the mentoring calls and man-to-man chats. You both helped me to think unlimited, strengthen my mindset, and stay the course.

Professor Crocker – you probably forgot who I am, but thanks for convincing me to apply to study abroad. That singular experience changed my life and opened my mind to the world.

Peace Corps – I have so much love for all the Volunteers I served alongside in Peru. Through the various ups and downs, we enjoyed some great times and made the world a better place.

James and Hugh – thanks for the mentorship and investing in me. Following in your footsteps, I am also paying it forward to support other people without asking for anything in return.

Tammy and Dory – thank you for your unwavering friendship. The endless support via WhatsApp messages truly helped me to get through various rough patches in my life.

Kary, David, and the Tribe – I truly appreciated all your support. This journey was indeed a team effort, and I am so thankful to be a part of this incredible group.

Annie and Denise – thanks for taking the time to carefully edit my book while maintaining its integrity and not cutting out my voice. You both made me a better writer and storyteller.

Introduction

Grateful and humbled, I returned to the United States after experiencing a transformational mind-altering and unforgettable adventure which forever changed my life. Never in my wildest dreams could I have imagined that I would leave everything behind, emigrate to a foreign country, and discover who I was meant to become.

Like a river, the content of this book flows spontaneously and organically straight from its source. Within these pages, you will get to know my personal story and the lessons I learned, which defined and transformed me into being the creative entrepreneur I am today.

I intentionally entitled this book *Burdens of a Dream* because I wanted to expose the hidden costs associated with embarking on the journey of entrepreneurship. The subtitle "33 Actionable Nuggets of Wisdom for the Creative Entrepreneur" is just what it sounds like: pieces of advice I culled from my experience.

Now, I'm sure you're wondering, *what exactly is a creative entrepreneur*? Well, this is a complicated question, and I too struggled with defining what these words meant to me. After endless self-questioning, I *created* my definition. To me, a creative entrepreneur is anyone who takes a calculated risk to create something out of nothing and share it with the world.

I recommend you read and analyze every chapter as an individual case study before moving onto the next. From there, apply your insights and lessons learned to circumvent inevitable obstacles, prevent self-sabotage, and optimize performance within your life.

Now, I leave you with the opening stanza from Robert Frost's "*The Road Not Taken*" to prepare your mind for what awaits you in the following pages:

Two roads diverged in a yellow wood,
And sorry I could not travel both
And be one traveler, long I stood
And looked down one as far as I could
To where it bent in the undergrowth.

01

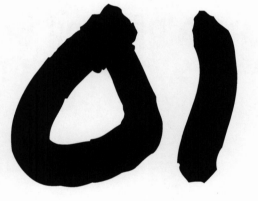

Change happens when the pain of staying the same is greater than the pain of change.

—Tony Robbins

Chapter 1: Growing Pains

My life drastically changed the moment I tore my hamstring while returning a punt during my sophomore year playing college football. After suffering this season-ending injury, I quickly entered a spiral of depression and contemplated dropping out of school.

For some mysterious reason, my Spanish professor intervened in my life and recommended I apply for a scholarship to study abroad in Costa Rica. Although, I gladly filled out the paperwork to make her happy, I quickly erased any hope of winning the award.

Serendipitously, one month later, I received an email confirming I won the scholarship plus a stipend to study abroad. Within a few months, I spoke conversational Spanish, was unexpectedly bit by the travel bug and became addicted to world travel.

Additionally, this experience also exposed me to the possibilities of living and working in another country. Upon returning from Costa Rica, I immediately switched my major to entrepreneurship, co-founded an e-commerce business, and invested the profits in studying abroad in Spain the following summer.

The creative entrepreneur views their present struggles as prerequisites for future success and resiliently fights through adversity. Personal development can be uncomfortable, and many people unfortunately remain stuck within their habitual and limited thought cycles. Stay vigilant for life's curveballs and never run away from the opportunity to grow into a better version of yourself.

02

If you don't design your own life plan, chances are you'll fall into someone else's plan. And guess what they have planned for you? Not much.

—Jim Rohn

Chapter 2: Decisions, Decisions, Decisions....

After obtaining my undergraduate degree, I decided to continue my education and earn my MBA before I entered the workforce. During my final semester of studies and only a few weeks before graduation, I started interviewing for various corporate jobs in New York City and San Francisco.

Throughout each interview, I observed the hiring managers suavely manipulating my young ego. According to them, I would "have a bright future, rapidly ascend through the organizational ranks, and enjoy a long-lasting career."

Although I enjoyed the business class flights, flattery, and upgraded hotel suites, my conscience warned me I would not enjoy working within these environments. Realizing this fact, I sought out other avenues and randomly connected with a Peace Corps recruiter at a local career fair.

Without hesitation, I willingly completed the arduous application, traversed the gauntlet of medical exams, and was invited to serve in Peru as a Community Economic Development Facilitator. With corporate America in the rearview mirror, I packed my bags and prepared for the oncoming adventure.

The creative entrepreneur defines their priorities, visualizes their future, and builds a plan to accomplish their goals. Recognize that some people will try to persuade you to make decisions on their terms and not in your best interests. Nobody else in the world can live your life, and it is up to you to make the most out of your current circumstances.

03

Creativity is the state of consciousness in which you enter into the treasury of your innermost being and bring the beauty into manifestation.

—Torkom Saraydarian

Chapter 3: M. A. G. I. C.

As the airplane departed from Washington, D.C, destined for Lima, Peru, I closed my eyes and envisioned myself as a successful international businessman. Even though I did not know how or if this dream would come true, I figured I'd take a chance to make it a reality.

The first weeks of Peace Corps training included language practice, various community activities, and learning from other Volunteers in the field. After hours, I spent time bonding with my host family, exploring the local markets, and working out with other people in my training group.

Often, at sunset, I walked to my little perch on the hill, looked down on my neighborhood, and meditated on my dream. Life was so different, and somedays I would freeze in amazement to question how I ended up in the middle of a developing country with a bunch of people who wanted to change the world.

Reminiscing on my experiences studying abroad in Costa Rica and Spain, I realized that I had arrived in Peru not by accident but by purpose. Two months later, I completed my training, swore an oath to serve as a Volunteer, and separated from my training group to venture out into the unknown.

The creative entrepreneur is a visionary that possesses the unique ability to manifest abstract goals into consciousness. Although the process of creation is not linear or logical, remember that ideas will forever remain ideas until you decide to make them a reality. Set your end destination, reverse engineer your path, and methodically execute until you accomplish your goals.

04

There are three principal means of acquiring knowledge... observation of nature, reflection, and experimentation. Observation collects facts; reflection combines them; experimentation verifies the result of that combination.

—Denis Diderot

Chapter 4: Pattern Recognition

After spending a few months acclimating to my new community and host family, I returned to Lima to spend the weekend exploring different parts of the city with other Volunteers. This place was a massive urban labyrinth where traffic was backed up for miles, exhaust from cars painted the buildings, and slums covered the hills as far as the eye could see.

We surfed in the cold waters of the Pacific, overdosed on fresh ceviche, and danced the night away in the clubs. During our last day in town, I sparked up a conversation with the owner of our hostel, and he suggested that I visit his brother's pisco distillery.

Unfamiliar with pisco, I decided to check the place out and burn some time before I returned to my community. When I arrived at the distillery, I learned that pisco was a nationally recognized spirit distilled from grapes that were grown in certain regions of Peru.

After a lengthy conversation with the owner, he discreetly mentioned that his business was rapidly expanding due to increasing demand from his customers. With this insight, I wrote down a few notes, bought a few bottles of pisco to share with my host family, and enjoyed a few sips during the 18-hour bus ride home.

The creative entrepreneur pays careful attention to their surroundings and logically analyzes situations to make informed decisions. Although many forms of information are easily accessible in today's world, do not expect the answers to your questions to majestically appear in front of your eyes. Leverage the keen power of observation to identify changes in human behavior, forecast new market trends, and position yourself for future success.

05

And the day came when the risk to remain tight in a bud was more painful than the risk it took to blossom.

—Anaïs Nin

Chapter 5: Discover Your Gifts

While drinking pisco with my host dad, he mentioned there was an opportunity to introduce higher quality versions of this product to the market. Furthermore, based on personal preference, some people preferred to drink pisco straight while others used it as a base to create homemade liqueurs.

These liqueurs were made from fruit, spices, or herbs that were soaked in pisco for various amounts of time. Next, the ingredients were strained, and sugars were added to make the final product.

As we drank the night away, I explained that as a child, I sucked on my fingers, and my mother tried using hot sauce as a deterrent. Her plan failed miserably, and because of these experiments, I gained the ability to eat spicy food and quickly identify new flavors.

Inspired by Italian limoncello, I began crafting liqueurs using local limes instead of lemon. Although my first batch of "limoncello Peruano" tasted like floor cleaner, the next batches tasted better as I leveraged my talent of taste to continually improve my recipes.

The creative entrepreneur must dig inside to find the confidence to conquer self-doubt and express their inner creativity. Recognize that work is an activity that consumes most of our energy, and it is advantageous to develop a business around your strengths. Focus on leveraging your natural gifts and always remember that hard work beats talent when talent does not work hard.

06

Start small, think big. Don't worry about too many things at once. Take a handful of simple things to begin with, and then progress to more complex ones. Think about not just tomorrow, but the future.

—Steve Jobs

Chapter 6: Start Where You Are

As mentioned, my first batches of liqueurs tasted awful; nevertheless, I continued to experiment and perfect my craft. One day after eating ceviche with a group of 10 farmers, I opened a reused and mysterious looking plastic bottle filled with my homemade concoction.

Knowing these farmers would drink just about anything, I figured they would be a perfect test group, and I poured out samples for everyone to try. As they threw back shots of my limoncello Peruano, I carefully observed their facial expressions and initial reactions.

To my astonishment, most of the farmers enjoyed it, and several of them asked for a second tasting. During this moment, a light suddenly went off in my mind, and the next day I designed a brief questionnaire to discover why they liked or disliked my product.

Although I knew this method of data collection could be flawed, I passed out questionnaires to all 10 of the farmers who participated in my test trial. Amazingly, 8 out of 10 farmers responded with positive feedback that further validated my product and inspired me to continue making my liqueur.

The creative entrepreneur prepares for opportunities, maximizes the current resources at their disposal, and acts without hesitation. Perfect timing is elusive, and the stars may never align to reveal the ideal moment to test your product, process, or service on potential customers. It's up to you to seize the day, squeeze the juice out of every moment, and transform lemons into lemonade.

07

A lot of people are all talk, what they say and what they do are two different things. As the saying goes, talk is cheap. Without actions behind the talk, it is all useless.

—Catherine Pulsifer

Chapter 7: Human Behavior Reveals All

Inspired by the success of my creation, I started thinking about additional flavors of liqueurs I could potentially offer in the future. Although my limoncello Peruano was a hit, I knew the market would eventually demand more variety.

Relying on my previous experiment, I casually asked the same group of 10 farmers to recommend a few additional flavors of liqueurs they would enjoy. Once the interviews ended, I had a list of more than 30 potential options and no idea how I could apply or use this information.

After analyzing the data, I realized the farmers couldn't respond honestly without tasting real samples. Inspired by this revelation, I created an assortment of random flavors of liqueurs and presented them to the farmers.

Through the careful observation of their actual behavioral responses, I identified which samples the farmers liked and disliked. From there, I added the top three flavors chosen by the farmers to my portfolio of new products.

The creative entrepreneur sees through the smokescreen of verbal language and recognizes that actions typically speak louder than words. Realize that it is common to obtain vague responses from people who are presented with open-ended or opinion-based questions. Avoid misleading data and ask behavioral-based questions to drastically increase the likelihood of receiving actionable insights from your research.

08

Entrepreneurs have a natural inclination to go it alone. While this do-it-yourself spirit can help you move forward, adding an element of collaboration into the mix can make you unstoppable.

—Leah Busque

Chapter 8: Collaborate + Elevate

As I was perfecting the various recipes for my liqueurs, I began using more and more pisco to fuel my operations. Dependent upon this resource, I started researching how to make it, but I had no clue where to begin.

Without notice, I received an invitation to collaborate with another Volunteer who lived in a different region of the country. We spoke for a few minutes, and she explained her plan to implement the youth entrepreneurship program at an agricultural institute where they produced wine and pisco.

Recognizing that moment as a golden opportunity, I immediately bought a bus ticket and traveled 20 hours through the mountains to reach her community. Once I arrived, my friend introduced me to a professor who also served as the institute's master distiller.

Over the next few days, we implemented the youth entrepreneurship program and helped several students to write business plans. In exchange for my work, the professor taught me how to distill pisco, shared his secret liqueur recipes, and accepted my request for continued mentorship.

The creative entrepreneur recognizes their limitations and willingly steps out of their comfort zone to learn from others. Understand that everybody's capabilities are limited because we all possess various strengths and weaknesses that define who we are. Avoid working in a vacuum and collaborate with others to foster innovation, expedite personal development, and gain access to unforeseen opportunities.

09

The great thing in life is efficiency. If you amount to anything in the world, your time is valuable, your energy precious. They are your success capital, and you cannot afford to heedlessly throw them away or trifle with them.

—Orison Swett Marden

Chapter 9: Processes for Profits

Feeling rejuvenated and energized from my work-exchange trip, I was ready to apply all the knowledge gained from my newfound mentor. After learning how to distill, my new priorities were cutting down waste and streamlining my production line.

At that time, I tediously hand-filtered, hand-bottled, and hand-labeled my liqueurs, which consumed a lot of precious time and energy. Even though I knew time was my most valuable resource, I was still trapped in the habit of performing and repeating the same algorithmic tasks.

To remedy the situation, I decided to sit down and map out my current operational processes to identify every bottleneck that slowed down the production line. Once the chokepoints were revealed, I started researching how to improve each process.

Later, I traveled to my regional capital and purchased a filtration machine, a bottle filler, and a semi-automatic labeler. Implementing these tools, I decreased waste, doubled production, and freed up my time to focus on developing a business plan for my distillery.

The creative entrepreneur bypasses the internal locus of control and reframes their mindset to eliminate the need to micromanage business activities. Realize establishing organized systems and processes helps to increase efficiency by reducing waste. Separate from the need to work "within your business" and instead work "on your business" to achieve optimal results.

10

For me life is continuously being hungry. The meaning of life is not simply to exist, to survive, but to move ahead, to go up, to achieve, to conquer.

—Arnold Schwarzenegger

Chapter 10: Purposefully Seeking Purpose

Living and working by yourself in a foreign country had its various pros and cons. However, I thrived within this setting and enjoyed the privilege to perform my job without much oversight.

During pre-service training, the facilitators emphasized that serving in the Peace Corps would be the "toughest job you'll ever love." Initially, I laughed at this statement, but as I found myself further entranced in my service, I slowly learned how to fall in love with my work.

Some days I worked in the blazing heat with farmers, other days, I taught students how to write a business plan, and sometimes I played catch with the knuckle-headed kids who lived on my street. There were hardly any dull moments, and each day was filled with excitement.

Through managing the expenditure of my time and energy, I established my definition of freedom and started living life on my terms. Reinvigorated by this discovery, I showed up to work every day with focus, a smile on my face, and the intent to create value for others.

The creative entrepreneur conducts a thorough self-analysis to discover their vision statement and live with purpose. Without any direction, you are guaranteed to wander around lost, waste time, and lose sight of your goals. Always remember to take a break, spend time with yourself, and never let fear prevent you from developing into the person you are meant to become.

”

Life is a storm, my young friend. You will bask in the sunlight one moment, be shattered on the rocks the next. What makes you a man is what you do when that storm comes.

—Alexandre Dumas

Chapter 11: Weather the Storms of Life

A typical work week serving in the Peace Corps contained both euphoric emotional highs and depressing emotional lows. Conditions were often extreme, and unpleasant situations commonly appeared out of thin air.

Within the same week I lost 15 pounds after contracting a mosquito-borne illness, was unlawfully detained by Peruvian police at a checkpoint located not far from my community, and unexpectedly moved into my own house because my host sister tried to stab me when I broke up a fight between her and my host mother.

After experiencing these hardships, my emotions were running rampant, and thoughts of doubt began to cloud my judgment. Life was crazy, and there were many days when I thought about handing in my two-weeks' notice, packing my bags, and booking a one-way ticket back to the States.

Fortunately, I remembered my dream of becoming a successful international businessman, and I realized that I had come too far within my journey. Declaring that quitting would not solve my problems, I decided to continue pursuing my goals of completing my service and opening a distillery.

The creative entrepreneur accepts challenges, resists the urge to quit, and perseveres through hard times. Running into difficulties in life is unavoidable, and you are guaranteed to experience many twists and turns within your journey of entrepreneurship. Control your energy, positively respond to adversity, and live to see another day.

12

As you grow older you will discover that you have two hands. One for helping yourself, the other for helping others.

—Audrey Hepburn

Chapter 12: Selfish + Selfless

Although I enjoyed some aspects of the laidback Peruvian work environment, it was tough adjusting to some aspects of the culture. *La Hora Peruana* was too real, and whenever I scheduled meetings, hardly anyone arrived on time.

Whenever I became frustrated, I reminded myself of the three goals of the Peace Corps:

1. Help the people of interested countries in meeting their need for trained men and women
2. Promote a better understanding of Americans on the part of the peoples served
3. Help promote a better understanding of other peoples on the part of Americans

Even though I was considered a leader and subject matter expert, to be successful in my work, I needed to adjust my way of thinking. As a way of adapting to the local culture, I scheduled meetings several hours in advance, knowing most people would show up late.

Ironically, some of my Peruvian counterparts that initially showed up late to meetings became raving fans and evangelists for my liqueurs. Ultimately, casting aside my ego to serve others helped to build trust and further cement my credibility within my community.

The creative entrepreneur places the collective over the individual and pays it forward to solve other people's problems. Everybody requires assistance in some shape or form, and it is worthwhile to view these situations as prime opportunities instead of mere inconveniences. Kill two birds with one stone by aligning your customer's best interests with your interests to create value for each stakeholder involved.

13

You must be the person you have never had the courage to be. Gradually, you will discover that you are that person, but until you can see this clearly, you must pretend and invent.

—Paulo Coelho

Chapter 13: Carpe Diem

As I was nearing the halfway point of my service commitment, waves of fear and doubt slowly crept into my mind. With only 12 months remaining, I needed to figure out my plan for life after the Peace Corps.

Most of the other Volunteers planned to apply to grad school, backpack through South America, or return home. Although the entrepreneur within me was screaming for an opportunity to resurface, I suppressed its calling to investigate other options.

Confused and unsure of what to do, I reached out to my trusted friends and family to discuss my plans and gather feedback. After mentioning my idea to open a distillery, everybody unanimously suggested that I stick to my guns and not give up on my dream.

For weeks I waffled back and forth, debating my future only to realize that running away from my dream would contaminate my soul with regret. Sensing this pain, I swallowed my pride and re-committed to manifesting my dream into reality.

The creative entrepreneur views their life as a continuous work in progress and embraces change as an essential phase of self-evolution. Understand that life often presents difficult choices, and indecisiveness may mislead you down a path full of regret, confusion, and despair. Remember, discomfort is only temporary, and the rewards of perseverance are worth their weight in gold.

14

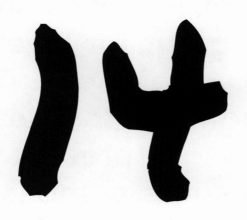

Life is hard enough without the added fear, panic and anxiety. Your soul is crying out for love and encouragement. Take a moment to breathe deep, get present and find some compassion for yourself.

—Jennifer Young

Chapter 14: Treat Yo' Self

After completing my youth entrepreneurship program and spending months reorganizing the local farming associations, I was mentally exhausted and worn out. Thankfully Christmas was rapidly approaching, and the entire country would soon shut down for several weeks.

In Peru, it is summertime in December, and many people flocked to the beaches to spend time with family and friends. I desperately needed a vacation, so I joined up with a few other Volunteers and escaped to the quaint beach town of Zorritos.

This place was otherworldly as time appeared to pass by at a slower pace while people worked to live instead of living to work. All inhibitions were castaway as we skinny-dipped among the fluorescent algae in the ocean, devoured freshly caught seafood from the local market, and fell asleep to crashing waves.

During our final night on the beach, we all sat around the campfire, shared a bottle of my liqueur, and openly discussed our inner struggles as Volunteers serving in the Peace Corps. Not wanting this moment to end, I hopped into my hammock, listened to the waves, and finally put my mind at ease.

The creative entrepreneur engages in self-care to proactively safeguard their mental and physical wellbeing. Although our professions make up just one facet of our existence, many people are regrettably enslaved to their jobs and breakdown as a result. Work hard, play hard, and do your best to maintain balance within your journey of entrepreneurship.

15

Maybe the most important reason for writing is to prevent the erosion of time so that memories will not be blown away by the wind. Write to register history, and name each thing. Write what should not be forgotten.

—Isabel Allende

Chapter 15: The Power of the Pen

Feeling rejuvenated after taking a much-needed vacation, I returned to my community and started a new round of projects. As my workload increased, I stopped making liqueurs and procrastinated with the idea of finalizing the business plan for my distillery.

By allowing sheer laziness to stop my momentum, waves of excuses crashed down and almost drowned any hope of progress. With my dream on life support, I ran toward the mirror, looked myself in the eye, and confronted myself.

Remembering the power of journaling, I bought a notebook and slowly began to capture my thoughts. Soon, unrelated and abstract concepts developed into actionable insights, which later formed into a concrete business plan.

I finally had my ideas cemented on paper and swiftly reentered my flow state to become more productive. Now with a restored focus and a new sense of direction, I gladly returned to working on my projects and making liqueurs.

The creative entrepreneur understands that journaling fosters self-motivation, clarifies priorities, and increases productivity. In life, our plans are guaranteed to incur some change, but you're forced to observe and evaluate each of them when they are written down. Do not rely on memory alone, buy a journal, and take the initiative to capture your thoughts on paper.

16

However desperate the situation and circumstances, don't despair. When there is everything to fear, be unafraid. When surrounded by dangers, fear none of them. When without resources, depend on resourcefulness.

—Sun Tzu

Chapter 16: Scarcity Fuels Resourcefulness

Like Clark Kent and Superman, I too developed an alter ego and transformed from a regular Peace Corps Volunteer during the day into a savvy bootlegger at night. Newly minted with the brand name Ponciana, I now presented my liqueurs in glass flask bottles covered with computer printed labels and clear masking tape.

Although the packaging was quite janky, the liqueurs grew in popularity as more people started requesting free samples. Visualizing the bigger picture, I desired to upgrade the image of my side hustle but lacked the resources to pay for these services.

Fortunately, I worked with a bunch of incredibly creative, uber-talented, and hardworking Volunteers. With a new plan in mind, I called another Volunteer who was a skilled graphic artist and brokered a deal to trade my labor in exchange for upgraded label designs.

From there, I traveled 24 hours by bus to her community, facilitated a business plan competition for her students, and received several label designs in return. A massive step up from the originals, the upgraded labels delivered a professional look and increased brand awareness for my liqueurs.

The creative entrepreneur has a mindset of abundance, and cleverly develops strategies to overcome difficulties. At some point within your entrepreneurial journey, you will be strapped for resources and forced to make decisions that will either push you forward or inhibit progress. Do not panic and use your mind to leverage your shortcomings, connect the dots, and locate alternative paths to reach your goals.

17

You don't have to achieve everything overnight. You just have to be willing to try. One day at a time. Just keep trying. Keep believing.

—Akiroq Brost

Chapter 17: Base Hits Outscore Home Runs

With a growing brand and solid business plan, I shifted my focus toward obtaining the capital I needed to open a distillery. Relying on my experience working with a variety of local small businesses as a point of reference, I estimated the startup costs to be around $20,000.

To complicate matters further, as a foreigner, I would have limited access to capital within the bureaucratic Peruvian financial system. Anticipating the difficulties to come, I brainstormed various strategies to raise money and eventually decided upon crowdfunding.

This method of raising capital was perfect because I could promote my distillery to an international audience and collect money from investors without giving up equity in my business. Believing this could be my path to success, I started researching past crowdfunding campaigns to discover why they failed or succeeded.

To expedite my learning, I reached out to the creators of various successful campaigns, asked for their help, and diligently listened to their advice. With this invaluable information, I established a timeline, set monthly benchmarks, and started executing my plan to launch a crowdfunding campaign.

The creative entrepreneur thinks over the long-term, is strategic, and persistently works toward the achievement of their goals. Although we live in a culture that promises instant gratification, sustainable results will not magically appear overnight. Understand that entrepreneurship is a war of attrition, and victory is only awarded to those who consistently win the smaller battles.

18

Corporations are not legal 'persons' with constitutional rights and freedoms of their own, but legal fictions that we created and must therefore control.

—Kalle Lasn

Chapter 18: Own Nothing, but Control Everything

Aside from teaching youth entrepreneurship, my second passion involved supporting local small business owners. No single business was the same as I worked with mom and pop grocery stores, family-owned restaurants, and farmers who sold produce at the local market.

Due to the intense Peruvian bureaucracy, many businesses did not formally register with the government, and tons of unregulated goods and services were sold to the public. Ironically, some of the people I knew owned businesses that were shut down by the government because they were not formally registered.

Not wanting to experience a similar fate, I began studying the local business laws to understand how I could formally open and register a business as a foreigner. Surprisingly, I learned that the government required all foreign business owners to have a Peruvian partner with a minimum of 1% ownership within the company.

Understanding my shortcomings, I asked a trusted friend who had both Peruvian and U.S. citizenship for assistance. After sampling my liqueurs and reviewing my business plan, he later agreed to become my silent business partner.

The creative entrepreneur leverages legal systems to display professionalism, maintain compliance, and hedge against risk. Currently, we live in a very litigious society where people are taken to court for petty infractions, personal vendettas, or simply breathing. Take advantage of the law and register your business to protect yourself and personal assets from harm.

19

The biggest challenge is to stay focused. It's to have the discipline when there are so many competing things.

—Alexa Hirschfeld

Chapter 19: Eyes on the Prize

As I approached the end of my service, my workload drastically increased as I was pressing through my final month as a Peace Corps Volunteer. With little free time, I struggled with balancing out my obligations to the Peace Corps and finalizing my crowdfunding plan.

Projects I used to enjoy suddenly transformed into annoyances as I rushed to turn in my closing reports. Stressed and worn out, I started slacking off and became unproductive.

After taking a few days to rest, I collected my thoughts, reorganized, and created a schedule that blocked out specific chunks of time for my work projects and side hustle. This new regimen kept me motivated and disciplined to execute various tasks at hand.

With my projects successfully closed out and transition plan in place, I enjoyed my last days in my community. After packing my bags and saying a sad goodbye to everybody I knew, I returned to Lima to finally close out my service.

The creative entrepreneur deliberately blocks out distractions and stays focused on solving their current problems. Know that your entrepreneurial journey is not a straightforward path, and there will be moments where you will wander astray and be tempted to quit. Stay proactive and create a plan that will point you in the right direction whenever you are lost.

20

It can be a grind, training and fighting and waiting for your chance. But when that opportunity presents itself, you have to be ready because you never know if or when you'll get another shot.

—Tyron Woodley

Chapter 20: The Point of No Return

The day I signed the paperwork to officially close out my Peace Corps service was filled with joy, relief, and trepidation. Although I was a free man, there were a few significant problems to resolve before I could move forward with opening my distillery.

To start the process, I was required to turn in my government visa, exit the country, and then return using my passport. From there, I had 180 days to work with a lawyer and my silent business partner to form a company and file immigration documents.

Ready to get this show on the road, I hopped on a plane and traveled back to the States for two weeks to spend time with my family. For a moment, I contemplated staying and looking for a 9 to 5 job until I reminisced over everything I accomplished.

As my mind raced through my memories, I stopped to reflect upon my dream to become a successful international businessman. Appreciating this once in a lifetime opportunity to open a distillery in Peru, I understood there would never be a better moment to manifest my dream.

The creative entrepreneur acknowledges their worries, transforms negative emotions into positive energy, and moves forward with conviction. No choice in life is truly risk free and uneasy feelings are a natural part of the decision-making progress. Although venturing into the unknown may be intimidating, never let fear stop you from moving forward in life.

21

What a person shows to the world is only one tiny facet of the iceberg hidden from sight. And more often than not, it's lined with cracks and scars that go all the way to the foundation of their soul.

—Sherrilyn Kenyon

Chapter 21: Trust, but Verify

I anxiously returned to Peru and was ready to begin filing the necessary business formation and immigration documents. To get the ball rolling, I reached out to several groups of American expatriates based in Lima and asked them for referrals to lawyers.

Ultimately, I narrowed my search down to two different options - a highly recommended and slick-haired senior lawyer versus a bright-eyed and freshly barred junior lawyer. I called both men to introduce myself and was impressed by the more experienced attorney's smooth demeanor and reputation.

Led by my emotions, I fell for the smooth-talking senior lawyer and agreed to work with him. The next day, the lawyer recommended that my silent business partner and I pay him in cash to expedite the processing for my company formation documents and work visa.

For reference, I called the junior lawyer to ask for his advice, and he was immediately suspicious of the cash payments. He recommended that I do not rush the process and graciously offered his support if I ever found myself in a bad situation.

The creative entrepreneur places little value on first impressions and takes their time to study a person's actual character. Sometimes reputation masks reality, and this false appearance could be hiding someone's real persona. Learn to develop your sense of discernment, and always trust your intuition when something doesn't feel right.

22

Never neglect small details, even to the point of being a pest. Moments of stress, confusion, and fatigue are exactly when mistakes happen. When everyone's mind is dulled or distracted the leader must be doubly vigilant.

—Colin Powell

Chapter 22: The Devil is in the Details

After filing the necessary business formation and immigration documents, I shifted my focus toward finding a suitable location for my distillery. While traveling around the country, I decided to set up shop in the northern beach town of Huanchaco.

This place was a popular tourist attraction famous for its surfing, hostels, and ceviche. Enjoying the vibes of this environment, I found this area to be ideal and swiftly moved into an apartment a few blocks from the beach.

Walking around town, I met a woman who lived on one of the main streets who was willing to rent out a two-story building attached to her family's house. With the summer tourist season rapidly approaching, I didn't have much time to sign a lease and open my distillery.

Unfamiliar with the local real estate process, I sent my lawyer a copy of the lease to review, and he said everything was good to sign. The next day, I rushed to meet the woman at her cousin's notary office, quickly signed the lease, and received the keys to the first floor of the building.

The creative entrepreneur carefully reviews their options and conducts the necessary research to make informed decisions. Although time is of the essence, mistakes are easily made whenever you are impatient and choose to ignore minor details. Remember to dot all your I's and cross all your T's before entering into a contractual agreement with another person.

23

Sweat equity is the most valuable equity there is. Know your business and industry better than anyone else in the world. Love what you do or don't do it.

—Mark Cuban

Chapter 23: Blood, Sweat, + Energy

Finally, with the keys in my pocket, I ran toward the beach and shouted with joy. Riding this roller coaster of exhilaration, I realized my dream was now a reality, and it was time to start putting in the real work.

Although the building was in decent shape, I had to clean up my entire space and design the layout for the distillery before I could begin the first round of construction. This process was not cheap, but thankfully, I saved most of the money from my Peace Corps readjustment allowance to pay for these expenses.

To cut back on costs, I vigorously scrubbed the floors, removed old tile, and painstakingly chipped paint off the walls. Though I was utterly exhausted, I cleaned like a madman, designed the layout for the distillery, and later received my building permit from the local municipality.

Now that my space was clean and stripped down to the bare bones, I hired a local contractor to begin the construction process. To celebrate, I took a few sips of my liqueur, spent the night in my building, and envisioned all the people who would come through my doors to enjoy my products.

The creative entrepreneur is completely dedicated to their craft and gladly makes the necessary sacrifices to stay the course. Nothing worth having comes easy and there may be times where you will be pressed to your known limits. Submit to the process, put forth your best efforts, and enjoy the fruits of your labor.

24

And the most successful people are those who accept and adapt to constant change. This adaptability requires a degree of flexibility and humility most people can't manage.

—Paul Lutus

Chapter 24: Go with the Flow

From my experience serving in the Peace Corps, I knew Peru and bureaucracy paired up together like peanut butter and jelly. Within this environment, outdated processes stifled simplicity, and basic tasks magically transformed into rocket science.

After contacting the local inspector to review the initial construction, several days passed without any returned calls or updates from his secretary. Time was not on my side, and instead of waiting on him day and night, I moved forward with the next task of opening a bank account for my distillery.

When I arrived at the bank, the manager demanded a signed copy of my business plan, along with a hand-written note from my landlord explaining the nature of my business. Resisting the urge to punch through a wall, I collected and submitted the necessary documentation, and waited several weeks for approval.

On the brink of losing my mind, I finally realized why so many of my former counterparts avoided working with government-owned banks. Now in limbo and at the mercy of the intricacies of the Peruvian financial system, I leveraged my free time and started executing my plan to launch my crowdfunding campaign.

The creative entrepreneur is versatile, quickly pivots, and easily changes direction to circumvent oncoming obstacles. On your journey of entrepreneurship, encountering setbacks are inevitable, but overthinking will only increase stress, doubt, and heartache. Accept the situation, make peace with your decisions, and let go of your need to control the outcome.

25

Hold up a mirror and ask yourself what you are capable of doing, and what you really care about. Then take the initiative - don't wait for someone else to ask you to act.

—Sylvia Earle

Chapter 25: Closed Mouths Don't Get Fed

With my bank account balance almost at zero, I had burned through my entire Peace Corps readjustment allowance and most of my savings. The time had finally arrived, and I was ready to execute my plan to raise the $20,000 I needed to open my distillery.

Thankfully I had a great support system, and my parents flew down to Peru to help me with my crowdfunding video. Working nonstop, we filmed everything in three days before I nervously shared the video with my entire network of friends and family.

As money slowly trickled in, I realized that my network was insufficient, and I needed to think quickly to find other people who would invest. Spontaneously, the next day, I cold-called the owners of seven minority-owned distilleries located back in the States and pitched them my story.

One out of the seven owners answered their phone and graciously invested a decent chunk of change into my crowdfunding campaign later that week. With this investment, I ultimately surpassed my initial goal and raised a total of $21,375 from 79 private investors.

The creative entrepreneur is aware of their limitations and willingly casts their pride aside to call out for help whenever they need it. Understand that working in silence may block the inflow of hidden opportunities and precious feedback from other people. Take note of the value you can provide, and do not be afraid to seek out assistance from those who can give it.

26

Unexpected events can set you back or set you up. It's all a matter of - perspective.

—Mary Anne Radmacher

Chapter 26: Murphy's Law

Basking in bliss with a successful crowdfunding campaign under my belt, I felt untouchable. After gaining some attention from the local media, I received a large number of pre-orders, and the local inspector finally confirmed his appointment to review the initial construction.

To prepare for his visit, I asked my contractor to double-check his work, and he told me everything would pass the inspection. The next day, the local inspector arrived with a stern face, walked through my door, and immediately stopped in front of the newly installed electrical distribution box.

Cold and emotionless, he stated that my building improvements violated code because the electrical system contained wires, which were several millimeters too thin. From there, he also said I could avoid future problems if I only bought and installed a new set of wires from him.

Although his price and demands were egregious, I succumbed and paid him off to dodge future problems. Shocked by this experience, I pushed forward and asked my contractor to start the final round of construction.

The creative entrepreneur hopes for the best and prepares for the worst to avoid the dangers of complacency. Sometimes life doesn't always flow according to our plans, and it is beneficial to anticipate the unexpected. Remember to listen to your conscience and leverage your inner compass to adjust whenever life throws you off course.

27

You need to be aware of what others are doing, applaud their efforts, acknowledge their successes, and encourage them in their pursuits. When we all help one another, everybody wins.

—Jim Stovall

Chapter 27: Leverage Strategic Partnerships

As my contractor was finishing construction, I moved onto the next phase of business, which included the development of my supply chain. Although I had an idea of where to begin, I couldn't find the right local merchants who could supply organic fruits for my liqueurs.

To my surprise, many vendors avoided wholesale orders, would only sell in small quantities, or could not deliver to my distillery. Frustrated and tired, I visited a local café to eat lunch and clear my mind.

After tasting the food, I asked to speak with the owner and was pleased to learn that she was also a foreigner. Over lunch, I expressed my struggles sourcing organic ingredients, and she graciously offered to connect me to her suppliers.

The following week, she helped me to negotiate prices with a few of her wholesalers and put in a big order of liqueurs to stock her bar. With no time to enjoy my little wins, I continued working non-stop while ignoring the blatant oncoming signs of mental and physical exhaustion.

The creative entrepreneur checks their ego at the door and teams up with others to develop mutually beneficial relationships. Realize that nobody is truly "self-made' and only narcissists believe they are successful exclusively based upon their merit. Avoid this trap and humble yourself by working with like-minded people to accelerate your learning curve and increase productivity.

28

Burnout occurs when your body and mind can no longer keep up with the tasks you demand of them. Don't try to force yourself to do the impossible. Delegate time for important tasks, but always be sure to leave time for relaxation and reflection.

—Del Suggs

Chapter 28: Burnout is Real

Sleep-deprived from working sixteen-hour shifts, I was running on fumes as I prepared to begin production on my first commercial batch of liqueurs. After purchasing a large amount of organic fruit, I contacted a local manufacturer to order a customized set of glass bottles.

Before this transaction was completed, I asked them to send the purchase order to my lawyer for verification and final approval. Later that week, almost a third of the fruit arrived spoiled, and half the shipment of bottles showed up either chipped or cracked.

On top of it all, my lawyer also sent me an outrageously overpriced bill for reviewing my lease and purchase order. Stressed out and frustrated, I fired several of my vendors, hastily hired a few employees, and aggressively micromanaged the entire production process.

Although I completed my first commercial fulfillment of liqueurs, I was drained of energy and barely hanging on by a thread. Entranced by the profits from sales, I continued to work long hours while careening toward complete burnout.

The creative entrepreneur equates health with wealth and values their mental wellbeing over material goods. A clear conscience is essential to longevity within your journey of entrepreneurship, and it is crucial to uphold a healthy work-life integration. Whenever you feel overworked, take the time to refocus, recharge, and rebuild yourself.

29

Things never go wrong at the moment you expect them to. When you're completely relaxed, oblivious to any potential dangers, that's when bad things happen.

—C.K. Kelly Martin

Chapter 29: Pay Attention to Subtle Warnings

Business was booming, my life was a blur, and the amount of free space in my distillery steadily shrunk as production increased. Not anticipating this surge of rapid growth before opening my distillery, I decided to review my lease contract and reexamine the details of the agreement.

With extra cash on hand and growing demand for my liqueurs, it made sense to exercise the option on my lease to rent out the additional space on the second floor of the building. Excited to present this news, I visited my landlord and shared my ambitions to expand my business.

The shell-shocked look on her face left me unsettled, and I returned home to rest my mind. That very night I experienced a paralyzing out-of-body experiential nightmare where I aimlessly wandered through a jungle, fell into a pit, and was viciously bitten by snakes.

Waking up, drenched in a pool of cold sweat, I had a bad feeling and realized something was wrong. The following day, I visited my landlord's house and was promptly notified that her older sister, who lived in Lima, was the actual owner of the property.

The creative entrepreneur listens to their intuition to carefully analyze their surroundings and identify oncoming threats. In a world full of deception, many warning signs appear in the subtlest of forms and regularly go undetected until the damage is done. Always trust your instincts and cease moving forward with decisions if you are uncertain or uncomfortable with the outcome.

30

Once you can tame your ego-mind, you are able to see clearly the path you were born to follow.

—Roxana Jones

Chapter 30: Ego Death

The pain from her deceit was quite vivid, and I struggled immensely with the fact that someone could lie, cheat, and steal without remorse. Ironically, only a few months prior, I enjoyed Christmas dinner with my supposed landlord and discussed how we could expand the distillery together.

After grasping the magnitude of the betrayal, I walked to the beach and reflected on what had transpired. The execution of the lease at a notary office owned by a close relative, extortion from the local inspector, and price gouging from my lawyer were all subtle signs of the impending doom.

Suddenly out of the blue, an epiphany struck my mind, which revealed a harsh and ugly truth. Unknowingly, serving in the Peace Corps for two years led me to falsely believe I was immune from the culture of corruption that was baked into the local business environment.

Although I was fluent in Spanish, I was not Peruvian and was entirely exposed to this hidden danger. Separating from my damaged self-identity, I collected my thoughts, crafted an excuse to avoid signing a new lease, and initiated my plan to exit the country.

The creative entrepreneur embraces their battle scars and discards any mental baggage that inhibits growth. Your journey of entrepreneurship will certainly hit a standstill, and your first instinct may be to wallow in self-pity and regret. Use pain as a tool to progress forward in life and never forget that a setback is a potential setup for future success.

31

If you're not failing, you're not pushing your limits, and if you're not pushing your limits, you're not maximizing your potential.

—Ray Dalio

CHAPTER 31: F. A. I. L.

A flood of sadness flowed through my mind as I looked out the bus window and gazed upon my former distillery for the last time. Holding onto a few cases of liqueurs, I felt like a complete failure because my dream was now a distant memory.

Out of the blue, endless questions appeared, and I kept asking myself, *how could I be left with nothing after giving so much of myself to this country?* Sensing an impending mental breakdown, I called several of my friends and family to ask for support.

Uplifted from their encouragement, I proudly declared that this temporary failure would not stop my hustle. Embracing the fact that things could have been a lot worse, I smiled and slowly began to calm down.

As I reminisced on my accomplishments, I realized that having the courage to finish the Peace Corps, emigrate back to Peru, and open a distillery was the epitome of success. This experience was only a first attempt in learning, and I was a stronger, wiser, and better man because of it.

The creative entrepreneur accepts the possibility of failure and maximizes the opportunity to learn from their mistakes. Some expectations may fall short of reality and there is always a chance you may not accomplish your goals. Weigh your options, take calculated risks, and remember decisions are what separates the doers from the dreamers.

32

Know from whence you came. If you know whence you came, there are absolutely no limitations to where you can go.

—James Baldwin

Chapter 32: Remember Who You Are

Although my landlord betrayed me, it was unfair of me to judge an entire country and culture based upon a separate lousy experience. To clear my head before I left Peru, I decided to return to my Peace Corps community one last time.

I figured I had nothing to lose, and I wanted to see if anything had changed since I closed out my service. Surprisingly, as I traversed through town, my mind immediately strolled down memory lane.

Not expecting much, I was amazed to witness several of my projects still being sustainably implemented by a few of my counterparts. Later, I visited my old host family, ate ceviche at my favorite local restaurant, and surprised my favorite group of farmers during their weekly reunion.

Finally, at peace with myself, I opened a bottle of liqueur and shared it with the original 10 farmers who first sampled my product. This time, instead of saying goodbye, I said, see you later, and calmly slept during my final bus ride back to Lima.

The creative entrepreneur outwits hardships, persists through the rigors of personal development, and refuses to run away from their dream. Creating something out of nothing is not easy, and it takes a lot of grit to endure the journey of entrepreneurship. Whenever you feel like all hope is lost, take a break to pause and reflect on just how far you have come.

33

Tomorrow is the most important thing in life. Comes into us at midnight very clean. It's perfect when it arrives and it puts itself in our hands. It hopes we've learned something from yesterday.

—John Wayne

Chapter 33: A New Hope

The moment the airplane departed from Lima, I was overcome with a sense of relief. Without a doubt, I fully embraced the person I saw reflected in the window and had zero regrets about the decisions I made.

Peru was officially in the past, and I finally had time to rest, heal, and recover. Eternally grateful for what came to pass, it was impossible to imagine my life without seizing the opportunity to manifest my dream into reality.

My time serving in the Peace Corps, and starting a business, trained me to think creatively, adapt to change and embrace the unknown. Each experience was priceless, and they both contributed to my personal development and transformation into a successful international businessman.

Although I did not know what tomorrow would bring, I knew I possessed the power to continue living a life full of purpose. My question today is, *do you*?

The creative entrepreneur learns from the past, takes massive action in the present, and optimistically strategizes for the future. Realize that life is an amalgamation of decisions, and the direction of your entrepreneurial journey is determined by the choices you make. Define what success means to you, choose to live life on your terms, and help make this world a better place for all.

How I started.

How I finished…

Conclusion

Ultimately, a simple decision can either serve as our best friend or worst enemy. I decided to embark on the journey of entrepreneurship, and I am still walking this path today. Once you choose to go down this road, you will be challenged and tempted to quit, but if you never give up and stay the course, you will transform into a higher version of yourself.

The only failure in life is failing to try, and never forget that you already possess the power to manifest your dream into reality. Your decisions determine your destiny and whenever you arrive at the next crossroads in your life, remember the closing stanza from "Robert Frost's "*The Road Not Taken*":

I shall be telling this with a sigh
Somewhere ages and ages hence:
Two roads diverged in a wood, and I—
I took the one less traveled by,
And that has made all the difference.

Sincerely,
Craig

Simply Scalable

The journey of entrepreneurship comes with its pluses and minuses, but the rewards surely outweigh the risks involved. There have been many times where I almost lost hope, had little money, or found a home sleeping on my sister's couch. But through hard work and dedication, I eventually regained my footing and overcame those *temporary* situations.

Today, I am a business coach that helps people live life on their terms through entrepreneurship. After years of trial and error, I developed a simple 12 step course that walks you through the entire process of conceiving, creating, and cultivating a scalable business.

Nothing worth having is easy, but as your coach, I'll be there to offer unconditional support once you decide this course is for you. Time is the one resource you can never get back, and this program is guaranteed to fast track your progress within your entrepreneurial journey.

Scan the QR code below using your phone or visit https://www.cre8ivecraig.com/simply-scalable to learn more:

Feedback

If you found any value in this book, please use your cell phone camera to scan the QR code below or visit https://www.cre8ivecraig.com/burdens-of-a-dream and leave a review:

About the Author

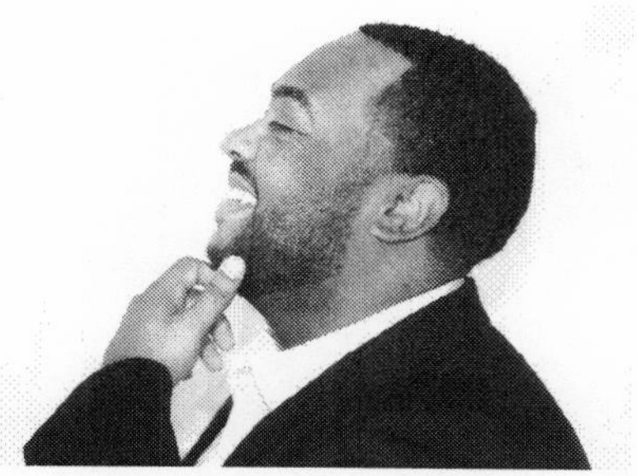

Craig is a serial entrepreneur with a deep and vast array of experience launching multiple global businesses based in Ghana, Peru, and the United States.

As a self-defined modern renaissance man, he enjoys cooking, traveling, reading, fashion, learning new languages, and anything else that piques his interest.

Craig sits on the boards of *Wild Goose Creative* and *Women in Technology International - Columbus*, serves as a *Forward Cities Innovation Sprint Mentor*, and is also an influencer within the Columbus, Ohio creative community.

If you would like to stay in touch, book a speaking/in-person engagement, or collaborate on a project, feel free to reach out and contact him via the following methods:

Cre8ive Craig

LinkedIn: www.linkedin.com/in/cre8ivecraig
Personal website: www.cre8ivecraig.com
Email: craig@cre8ivecraig.com
Instagram: @cre8ivecraig

Made in the USA
Monee, IL
27 March 2020

24027617R00092